Let's-Read-and-Find-Out Science®

Air Is All Around You

REVISED EDITION

by Franklyn M. Branley · illustrated by Holly Keller

HOUGHTON MIFFLIN

Boston · Atlanta · Dallas · Denver · Geneva, Illinois · Palo Alto · Princeton

The *Let's-Read-and-Find-Out Science* book series was originated by Dr. Franklyn M. Branley, Astronomer Emeritus and former Chairman of the American Museum–Hayden Planetarium, and was formerly co-edited by him and Dr. Roma Gans, Professor Emeritus of Childhood Education, Teachers College, Columbia University. Text and illustrations for each book in the series are checked for accuracy by an expert in the relevant field. For a complete catalog of Let's-Read-and-Find-Out Science books, write to HarperCollins Children's Books, 10 East 53rd Street, New York, NY 10022.

Library of Congress Cataloging-in-Publication Data
Branley, Franklyn Mansfield, 1915–
    Air is all around you.
    (Let's-read-and-find-out science. Stage 1)
    Summary: Describes the various properties of air and shows how to prove that air takes up space and that there is air dissolved in water.
    1. Air—Juvenile literature.   [1. Air]   I. Keller, Holly, ill.
II. Title.   III. Series.
QC161.2B7 1986   551.5   85-47884
ISBN 0-690-04502-6.—ISBN 0-690-04503-4 (lib. bdg.)
ISBN 0-06-445048-1 (pbk.)   85-45405

Revised edition

Air is all around you.

There is air down in a deep valley.

There is air around a high mountain.

Wherever you go, there is air.

Cars and houses are filled with it. So are barns, sheds, doghouses and birdhouses.

Cups are full of it. So are bowls, pots and glasses that we drink out of.

That's hard to believe because you can't see the air, or smell it. You can't feel it either, except when it's moving. Or when you spin around.

You can't see the air in a glass, but you can prove it is there. Try this experiment.

Run a lot of water into the sink. Or put water in
a big bowl. Color the water with a little food coloring.
Not much, just enough to color it a little bit.

Stuff a paper napkin into the bottom of a glass.
Turn the glass upside down. If the napkin falls out,
stuff it in tighter.

Keep the glass upside down. Make sure it is straight up and down. Do not tip it. Push it all the way under the water. Or as far under as you can.

Lift the glass out of the water. Turn it right side up and take out the paper napkin. It is dry. The water did not touch it. The paper was under the water. But it did not get wet. Let's see why.

Once again put the napkin in the glass. Turn
the glass upside down, and push it under the water.

Look at the glass through the water. The water
does not go into it.

It can't go in because there is air in the glass.

But you can make the water go in.

Tip the glass a little bit. A bubble of air goes out and up.

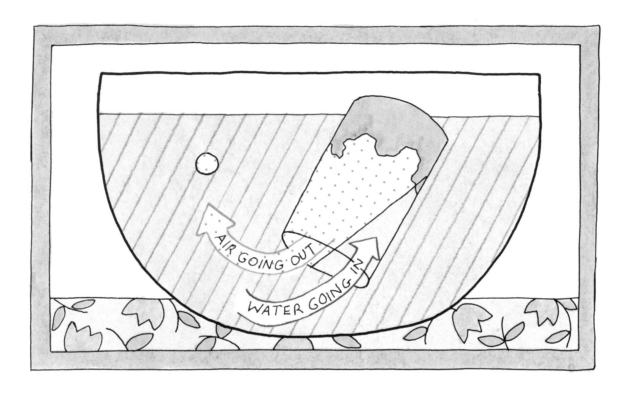

When the air goes out, there is empty space in the glass. Water goes in.

You can see it. The coloring you added to the water helps you see it. Bubbles go out, and water goes in.

Keep tipping the glass until all the air goes out.
Now it is full of water and the napkin is soaking wet.

When the glass was full of air, there was no
room for water. When the air went out, the water
went in.

Air is all around you, and it is all around the earth. Air covers the earth like peel covers an orange.

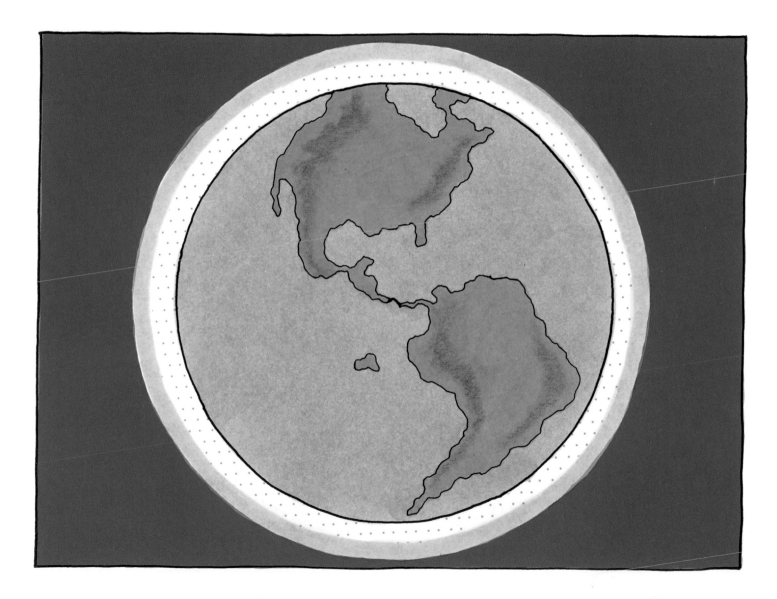

The air weighs a lot—5 quadrillion tons. That's 5,000,000,000,000,000 tons. That's hard to believe, but it's true.

The air in the room where you are weighs more than you think. In an average room, the air weighs seventy-five pounds or so. If the room is big, the air in it weighs more. If it is small, the air weighs less.
We don't feel it because the air is spread all around us.

Airplanes and balloons fly in the air. But spaceships don't. Rockets push them higher than the air. Spaceships fly above the air that is all around the earth.

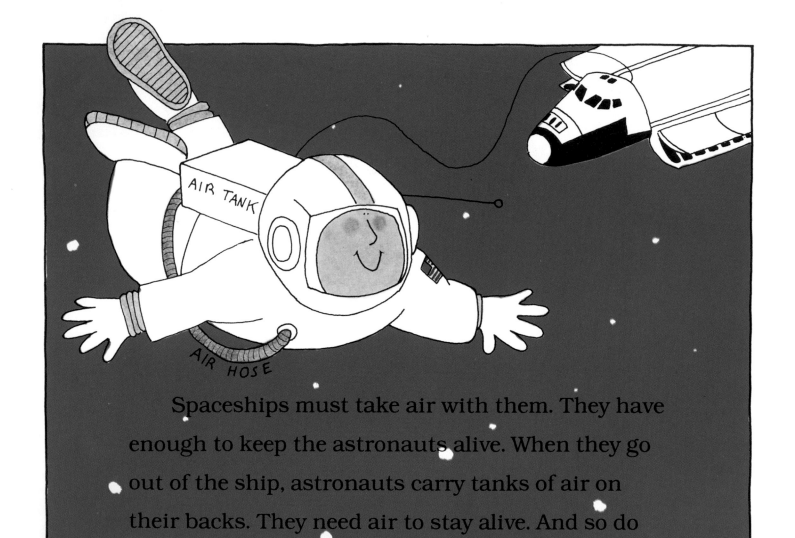

Spaceships must take air with them. They have enough to keep the astronauts alive. When they go out of the ship, astronauts carry tanks of air on their backs. They need air to stay alive. And so do you and I.

Lucky for us, air is everywhere. Wherever we go on earth, there is air. Air is even in water. That's lucky for fish. The air is dissolved in the water. You can't see the air. But you can prove that it is there.

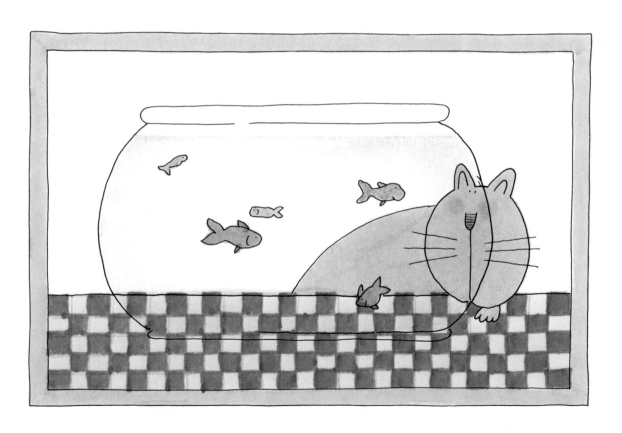

Fill a glass with water. Set the glass aside and leave it for an hour.

After an hour you will see little bubbles on the inside of the glass. They are tiny bubbles of air. The air came out of the water.

Fish use the air that is dissolved in water.

They have gills that help them do this.

Air keeps them alive.

We can't breathe air that is dissolved in water.
So when we stay under water a long time, we have
to take air with us. Divers take air in tanks
strapped to their backs.

AIR TANK

Air keeps us alive.

Wherever we go on earth—north, south, east or west, high on a mountain or deep in a valley—there is air.

Air is all around us.